DIVORCED AFTER 56 YEARS

WHY AM I SOOO HAPPY?

BRENDA FRANK

SUGAR GROVE PRESS

WHAT PEOPLE ARE SAYING

Wonderful, a modern declaration of independence!

Dr. Judie Manulkin, PHD

Hi Brenda,

I want you to know that I think your book is excellent. I'm pretty much going through the same thing right now. I lost my husband three months ago. I'm enjoying my Independence right now. I don't have to account to anyone for anything. I forwarded it to my two Granddaughters, who are making much more than their husbands. I hope they understand what you went through. Thank you for sending it to me.

Ann

Dear Brenda,

Thank you for sharing with me. I like the way its written - informal and friendly while dealing with a very difficult subject. I realize that using the "primer" approach is a good one, yet I feel that this could be developed into a memoir.

Shael

Brenda,

Loved your Primer and feel that it will talk to many and reach them.... What a great movie and Diane Keaton should play you. 56 years was a lifetime...you were a duo for more years of your life than the years of "freedom" and letting Brenda grow and glow!! Keep on trucking the horizons are limitless. You paid a price greater than most because of all the years invested and then the loss. You are doing a service for many.

Gigi

Brenda,

So we both read the Primer from cover to cover, and as John constantly reminds me, I never read anything other than email and industry magazines. Talk about an attention keeper..... I couldn't put it down until I finished it last night. We LOVE your writing style and can't believe this is the first thing that you've written!

Tom and John

Hey Brenda,

I just finished the primer. What a delight! The tempo is great and you interspersed great advice in a light way. I loved it!

Lisa

Brenda,

Loved the Primer. You certainly have a very unique and clever style of writing. It was as if I were in the same room with you talking one on one. Loved the different captions and photos as well. They just added to the demeanor of the subject matter. I am happy and proud of you for what you are doing.

Toby

CONTENTS

SUGAR GROVE PRESS

Published in the United States by Sugar Grove Press
an imprint of Sugar Grove Media LLC
Pompano Beach, Florida 33062
http://www.sugargrovepress.com

2nd printing edition 2021

Divorced After 56 Years Why Am I Sooo Happy? / Brenda Frank & r. h. krishen
Cover Design by Alfie Frohman
Cover photo by Barbara Frohman
Back cover photo by Bette Marshall

Paperback ISBN: 978-1-7368447-2-4
Library of Congress Control Number: 2021938703

DEDICATION

R. Thank you. You turned my virtual into reality. B.

INTRODUCTION

This is, by definition, not a book, but a primer. A *Primer,* (that's pronounced prim-err) *is an elementary textbook that serves as an introduction to a subject of study.* It is my mission to help you *go with the flow* rather than see you *sitting and stewing.* This is not a large book, I will begin at the beginning of the story that I'm telling, and I want you, my newest friend to read along with me.

"You've been served!" New Year's Eve 2014, these are the words forever frozen in my mind. So began my: dissolution, realization, revolution, and resolution. Happy New Year 2015.

I liken my recently ended marriage to a new jar of fresh, creamy peanut butter. "How can that be?" you ask. Don't you see the similarities? Well, when you open the jar, you take what you need with the butter knife and everything stays fresh and tidy. As you get deeper into the jar, it starts to get messy with gobs of peanut butter sticking to the sides. When you get to the bottom, you scrape the remains out with a spoon, and finally when it's almost empty, you put your finger in the jar, wipe it clean, lick your fingers, and throw away or re-cycle the jar.

You have used it all up, there is nothing but memories left. You have come to the end of the peanut butter and in the case of some marriages, especially the very long ones, it's the end of that too. Now it's time to lick your wounds and start fresh.

GRANDMA MOSES

I will never be a Grandma Moses. The closest I'll ever come is being a Grandma who never dozes. The grand Gram M was seventy, five years younger than I am, when she picked up a paint brush and became internationally famous. I turned on the computer, and lo and behold I discovered Word, spell-check, and a plethora of squiggly red and blue lines. I learned how to cut and paste. These have become the new tools and nomenclature of my trade. I now envision myself as a writer. No matter what other kind of work I ever involve myself in, I will write. My newfound purpose in life is to share information and inspire others to act.

WHERE DO I BEGIN? YOUR NEW LIFE BEGINS WITH THE LETTER "I".

Dear reader. I dedicate this book to you. By reading it, I hope it encourages you to understand yourself, helps you make positive changes, and aids you in coming to fully understand the most important person in your life is you, regardless of what you believe others may be thinking.

This is the founding of a new day, a re-birth, so let's get on with the show. I have a new status and definition of who I am. Today I am a writer. I want to retire my forty plus year's stint as a Realtor. By writing this, and by others reading it, if one individual's life is changed for the better, I have done my job. This can be you. If, though, by chance, your life changes for the worse, I deny any or all culpability.

I want you to know you have a sense of worth, you are valuable, you are needed, wanted, and most importantly, should feel good about yourself. You do not need anybody else to depend on for your happiness. You definitely don't need anyone to tell you that you can or cannot accomplish something that you daydreamed about and didn't have the confidence to try. If that comes to pass, and it should from reading and heeding my words, then it was worth the pain that goes into creating something meaningful and essential to your new significance of well-being.

If it's up, put it down. If it's always on the right, then put it on the left. Whatever you decide to do, you must concentrate on making a number of things in your life change. Altering long-standing habits are going to be difficult in the beginning, but it will become easier than you might think.

Above all, do not kill yourself doing it; it's not worth it. Make changes in small increments and treat yourself; give yourself a reward. It's not where you start; it's where you are and where you are going. A song from the play, *Seesaw,* states, *"It's not where you start, it's where you finish"*, and ends with, "A*nd you're gonna finish on top"!* That is where you need to be... on top!

FIRST MEETING

"The party's over, it's time to call it a day...it's over my friend", so laments the love interest in the 1956 Broadway musical, *The Music Man.* That was the year before the "F***ing Love of My Life" (heretofore to be referred to as "FLOML") walked into my life.

West Hartford, Connecticut. I was a junior in high school. March 1957, most fittingly, sometime around the Ides of March. (Maybe I should have studied Julius Caesar a bit closer). I was having lunch in the school cafeteria, when someone caught my eye, fresh blood, a new boy in school. He was in the food line, his long blond hair over his pulled-up shirt collar, chino pants, and sporting a khaki jacket was a far different look from local boys with their clipped short haircuts, buttoned up shirts, and oxford laced shoes.

Certainly, no one would dare wear an outer jacket indoors, especially in school. No one had a clue what his feet were clad in and I only found out later they were called *desert boots*.

Curious, my two friends, Linda and Judie, turned to see who I was staring at. Unbeknownst to me, they knew all about this guy who had the looks of Tab Hunter and the attitude of James Dean. I said, as I continued eating my Beef-aroni, "He's cute, too bad he's not Jewish". My friends exclaimed, in unison, "But, he is!" Now, my interest piqued.

They knew his name and that he had originally lived in Hartford. Three years before, his family moved to San Francisco, because of his father's job. Recently, though, the family relocated once again, this time to Boston.

Boston was only a few hours' drive from Hartford, and since he had friends from living there before, it was decided that he would live with his aunt and uncle in West Hartford and go to school there rather than start in a new school in Boston. He was in his senior year of high school. Days passed, and I did not see him again until our unexpected meeting in Judie's basement, aka the RecRoom, where anything and everything happened. (In those days, that meant not much!)

It was Friday night and there were the usual group of guys and gals hanging out listening to music on the juke box, flirting with each other, and since most of us were sixteen, an acceptable age to smoke at that time, smoking cigarettes.

The following day, I was going to an Iota Phi sorority convention in Boston, so I left Judie's get-together earlier than usual. As I was climbing the stairs I looked up, and near the top, there he was, the great looking guy from the school cafeteria coming down. Our eyes locked and he turned around and followed me up the stairs into the kitchen. "Hi", he said. "Hi", I said, and that was the opening salvo to a relationship that would last more than fifty-seven years.

Both of us being tongue tied made for very small talk. I told him I was going to Boston early the next morning. Reluctantly, I left. I said good night, excited that we had made the connection that started our journey together. That was in March 1957, and lasted until the day he left, Aug. 26, 2014.

IN THE BEGINNING

In the late 1950's, a girl had one of two descriptions: fast or good. The fast girls got lots of dates and the good girls, well, practiced safe sex our way; we got married. Much later I learned how right Woody Allen was when he said, "Sex without love is an empty experience, but as empty experiences go, it is one of the best".

Our wedding was in the gymatorium of the Beth David Synagogue in West Hartford, on Sept. 7th, 1958. It was a dismal, cool, drizzly Sunday evening. The cantor asked the rabbi, as he was walking down the rose petal strewn aisle to take his vows, if the young man was attending his Bar Mitzvah or his wedding, and if the groom was old enough to drive his new wife home. He looked more like a fourteen-year-old in need of a haircut, than a nineteen-year-old, soon to be, husband. This fact was emphasized even more by his ill-fitting, rented, white dinner jacket and black tuxedo pants.

I'm not certain if the damp, rainy weather made it droop, but what I still see in my mind is our lopsided wedding cake. The little plaster groom that looked like Clark Gable, sans mustache, and a blonde Japanese bride stuck to his side, stood wonky and conspicuously askew atop the third tier of the wedding cake, which was held up by a white plastic shelf, supported by three swans.

Leading up to the ceremony, my mother had pressed us to honeymoon in Miami Beach, rather than the Catskills, another favorite honeymoon destination. Her pearls of wisdom were, "If you don't go now you will never go". As it turned out, it was 20 years before I went to the Catskills, while racking up decades of Florida living.

Our first residence as husband and wife was a studio apartment in the back of a late 1800's apartment building at 1470 Beacon St., Brookline, Mass. We furnished it with my in-laws old, but still serviceable hi-rise bed, two chairs we had purchased ourselves, and a humongous table model TV that my father, who owned an appliance store, had repossessed from one of his customers no longer making the payments. The TV only got one channel. No wonder he stopped paying for it.

The Samsonite card table and chairs acquired with the nine books of S+H green stamps that my mother had earned by auspiciously grocery shopping on double stamp days was just the right size for our small kitchen. Minute Rice and canned stewed tomatoes was the first meal I made as a married woman of eighteen. We had dinner while sitting on our bed/sofa, at my new ironing board which functioned tonight as our dining table.

Fast forward 56 years to December 31, 2014. Happy New Year! I was served divorce papers!

COMPUTER LESSON

I remember the day of reckoning. I knew I had to learn how to use, that clunky TV-wannabe looking box called a computer. Sitting on the desk, it was daunting, and teased me to "come over and see me sometimes", daring me to see what all the hullabaloo was about. Little did I know that I would soon learn the difference between software and hardware is you can kick hardware.

I don't like change, and I never read directions. Now the world of computers was gaining on me, infringing into my life, and I was losing the race to fend off the inevitable. In order to survive in business, I had no choice but to learn how to master, or at least make friends with the computer. They are much like lawyers in one respect. You hate them until you need them...and then you still hate them. Many attempts on my own had failed miserably. After numerous starts and stops I knew I had to capitulate and seek help.

By this point in our relationship, the last person I wanted lessons from was him, but I didn't know who else to ask, and he was handy. He was somewhat computer savvy at the time. He figured out how he could keep me from reading his e-mails: he named his mail folder, *Instruction Manuals.*

He was the chosen one, due to a process of elimination. He also agreed to the ground rules I set. He asked where I wanted him to sit. *Idaho,* I thought. He settled on the couch, behind me, on the other side of the room, about twelve feet away. He was to patiently and calmly introduce me to the world of cyberspace without heavy breathing, sighing, or head shaking when I was unable to immediately grasp what he was explaining.

We worked on a practice document. I began to type, and my first question to him brought forth his answer of "press enter". You need to think back to the dark ages of computers, some 20 years ago. There was no key that said *enter.* The key on the right side of the keyboard, at the end of the middle row, said return. I was not about to give up. I continued looking for the word "enter".

"I can hear you," I said of hubby's heavy breathing, which didn't help matters.

"Press *enter,*" he bellowed.

My search continued, looking for the word, enter. A few minutes passed.

"Let me show you," he grimaced between clenched teeth and pursed lips.

"No," I cried.

My mind started to wander, and I wondered if after pleading justifiable homicide, how many years I'd spend in prison for killing him? I recently thought about that and realized that I probably would have been released by now, by an empathetic judge.

Finally, after punching every key that did not have a letter of the alphabet embossed on it, something happened. The secret to enter and moving to the next line was revealed by punching the word *return*. I must not have been the only person who pulled their hair out looking for *Enter*, because *Return* has been permanently Deleted. If some of these computers were designed by women, I'm sure they would be easier to understand. One thing's for certain, they couldn't be any more complicated.

Another argument ensued when his instruction was, "Press any key". I did ask, and received the now obvious answer, so that brainteaser was quickly abated. We continued with the session, although the environment was getting hot and heavy, and not in a sexual way. It appeared to me we were making some headway, until my next meltdown.

He continued to control himself with his heavy breathing, which in retrospect was probably healthier than barely breathing. I felt sorry for him...almost. I, on the other hand, wanted to throw the fucker...not him, the "puter", over the balcony of our fifteenth-floor condo and call it a day. Okay, okay...both of them.

He instructed me to "right click". I did. Nothing happened. I accused him, not too kindly, of not being as smart as he thought he was.

He repeated the command, "Right click."

I typed, typed, typed . . . nothing. He begged to come close to see what I was doing, but I turned to him with daggers in my eyes, and he remained seated. He cowered on the couch until I turned back to the computer. Frustrated, I made a third, and what I thought would be my last attempt to make something happen, but alas, to no avail. I was miserable and frustrated, but most of all, defeated. I didn't know whether to cry or kill. One more valiant effort was tried, with the same results.

"Tell me EXACTLY what you are doing," he snarled.

"What you are telling me to do," I snapped.

"I am telling you to 'right' click. Tell me, step by step exactly what you are doing," he pleaded, usurped of all patience.

I repeated in an 'I gottcha' voice.' "I am doing EXACTLY what you are telling me to do."

He collapsed in a heap on the couch incoherently muttering under his breath when I repeated his instructions articulating every word and letter step by step.

"I am writing c-l-i-c-k."

It wasn't that much later, after my computer lesson, that he suffered a heart attack requiring quadruple bypass surgery. And so began the unraveling of a 56-year marriage.

FLOML LEAVING

He left on August 26, 2014. "That's the last straw! I'm outta here!" were his parting words as he stormed out the door and ended our marriage. He was irate because I refused to agree to sell a piece of our real estate. I didn't see him again until he sauntered in for an uninvited visit in the beginning of November.

I had just returned from a trip to Morocco, which I had planned months before his unexpected exodus. I naively thought he was interested in hearing about my trip, but no, he came to share that he had flown, first class of course, to San Francisco for the World Series. One more scratch off on his bucket list.

One afternoon, shortly after, I was cleaning out his bathroom medicine cabinet, which he had mostly emptied when he left. Sitting at eye level, on the middle shelf, so as not to be missed, was an unfolded fortune from a fortune cookie. The message read, *your secret desire to completely change your life will manifest.* Hmm...did he leave it intentionally for me to read, or is that what made him decide to leave?

It was left behind when he took his personal belongings. The irony of that message has morphed itself to me, although at that time I didn't know I had secret desires going forward.

I learned the expression *give a hug, get a hug* is not altogether true. As he was leaving, after we shared our latest personal adventure stories, I went to him and gave him a hug, but his arms, which were by his side, stayed by his side, as if nail gunned to his hips. Oh well, adios to you, too!

Other than seeing him from afar at our mediation, where we did not share the same space, I have not seen him again. He went in with his lawyer while I sat in the lobby with my lawyer. I drifted off into a cat nap while waiting, imagining the conversation that was going on in there.

FLOML-"So, what can we take her for?"

His lawyer- "What's she got?"

FLOML- "Well, she works her ass off, and sells lots of real estate. I want half of everything she makes."

His Lawyer- (chuckling out loud) "Half? What are you, an under-achiever? She's been supporting you for ten years. You need to maintain that standard of living without her now. We can get 75%."

FLOML- (grinning from ear to ear) "Well," quoting the Nike ad, "Just Do It!"

I awoke from my nightmare in a sweat. We switched places as the afternoon dragged on. After spending tens of thousands of dollars for attorney's fees, I was coerced into an agreement. He was given 75% of our portfolio, and our Miami Beach condo, which was bought with money inherited by my parents.

They must be spinning in their graves over this debacle! I received 25% of our portfolio, the condo I live in, and two investment properties in Hollywood, Florida. Unfortunately, sometimes, dreams, or in this case nightmares, do come true. I was allowed to keep one investment mutual investment mutual fund inherited from my parents.

Early on, when he and I were still communicating by e-mails and texts, he exclaimed, after I told him he was not entitled to these mutual funds "...and I'm getting those, too!" Much to his chagrin, he did not. Fortunately for me, he missed co-mingling this account, so it did not become marital funds. He was shut out. Nice try, but tough luck!

He fought long and hard for his perceived pound of flesh. The irony was, that prior to his final departure, he always told me that if and when he ever left, all he would want were his jeans, a few shirts, and $250,000 which, in time, became $300,000, and in reality, finally 75% of our community property. It appears that divorce lawyers and judges are quite generous when it comes to other people's money.

I was no longer the beneficiary of his life insurance, as well as eliminated as a recipient of his pension. To add insult to injury, I had been the primary breadwinner for more than ten years as he lolled in the comforts of retirement.

I got penalized for working. After I informed my attorney I was planning on quitting, he exclaimed, "No, you can't do that, you can't change your lifestyle!" even though he had been beseeching me to do just that for at least the past few years. I was reprimanded for even considering retirement. I was told I must continue working. When I cried out, "why can't he work?" The asshole judge responded, "Because he hasn't worked in ten years, why should he start now?" *How about, because I'm not his fucking mother,* I thought. I was then reminded how lucky I was that Mr. Nice Guy was not going to ask for alimony. Lucky? I felt about as lucky as Tsutomu Yamaguchi, the only man who had the misfortune of being in both Hiroshima and Nagasaki when they were bombed in WWII.

My income had been paying his life insurance premiums and now I would be shut out of any possible benefits or pension income: Yup, guess you can call that luck! I had most assuredly been unfriended.

Note to anyone considering becoming a committee of one: I strongly advise you to consult with at least one attorney, if not a few, and an accountant, to best protect your ass-ets. You do not have to give away the store if you know the rules of the jungle, which I did not.

He enjoyed his golfing once or twice a week, and of course golf is even better with a brand-new set of Taylor-Made clubs and a personalized bag, instead of his ancient two-year-old, out of style Callaway's.

For his seventy-fifth birthday, in March, five months before his final exit, he crossed off one more bucket list item. We celebrated his big day with me watching him tee off at Pebble Beach. His retirement was as good as it gets. On my birthday, two days after his, I celebrated by showing up at my office and initiating my forty-first year of selling real estate. Well, if not me supporting his lifestyle, then whom?

He was the only love in my life from our meeting in March of 1957. We married in September 1958.That year and a half was an exciting and wonderful time for me. After we married, we struggled as many other couples did. We had some good times and raised two boys regardless of the fact that there were no how-to books that we could afford to buy, to help us. In spite of our lack of nurturing, they grew up and out and became successful men.

The road we took was often bumpy, sometime sunny, and sometimes gloomy. Near the end of our fifty-six-year journey we reached a crossroads.

I went one way, he went another. I must say that when all was said and done, if he did have a bucket list, it must've been pretty well completed, from marrying me, his high school sweetheart, to having two successful sons, climbing the corporate ladder, and traveling the world. His extra marital affair, twenty years into our marriage, which he confessed to me after he decided to stay, strengthened our resolve to make the renewal of our relationship stronger, which it did, and held for many years.

He retired from business in 1997. Soon, a 60+ age itch set in. During his retirement he took sailing lessons and then bought a boat, a speed boat. I should have taken golf lessons, and then bought a tennis racket! He tired of the speedboat within a year and proceeded to have a sailboat built, presumably because none of the sailboats already built were of his liking.

This was done after exclaiming, "Don't be ridiculous" to think that he was having a boat constructed. I questioned him about it when I was dusting the desk and happened see the computer monitor displaying dialogue between himself and a stranger named Bob, who was quite animated about how the boat building was going. FLOML continued with a straight face, "The guy is crazy, and I am definitely not having a boat built". The *crazy* man delivered the boat that he was definitely not building a month later. He even had the name picked out. I would have named it DEFINITELY (K)NOT; just another hint of things to come, that I missed.

Our relationship was fraying like an old elbow patched corduroy jacket. He became critical of and resented my continuing to work, although he did not hesitate to spend the money I was earning. He turned our marriage partnership into a competition of which he was the only competitor.

If I spent, he felt compelled to spend. Even though he left at the end of August, he continued to charge all of his expenses to our common credit cards. At the end of October, he charged over $8,000, flying first class to San Francisco for a one week stay, going to a World Series game, and taking others to dinner. Who did he take, the starting nine? He walked out of our marriage just prior to our fifty-sixth anniversary, having had enough of being married. I now look at divorce as a declaration of independence but with only two signers.

In January, I received, and for the first time looked at the yearly AMEX and Master Card *end of the year* report of our charges. It was only then I realized he was not just entertaining himself. I saw that he was entertaining numerous others. When I questioned him, after he had me served divorce papers on New Year's Eve, about those expenses, he said he went to some of these establishments to drink...alone.

When I got home at night from work, he never showed any hint of alcohol induced behavior, nor did he ever smell of liquor. If he was telling the truth, maybe it was Pepsi he was getting high on. Fifty-six years, and the only thing I could think to ask, if he had been around, was *WHO are you?*

Our friends would ask him, "What do you do all day?" as a way to compare how their own days measured up. Besides playing golf or going out on one of his boats, he would tell them that he watched TV or read. Yeah, OK, that's what he wanted others to believe.

As Helen Rowland so succinctly put it, "When two people decide to get a divorce, it isn't a sign that they don't understand one another, but a sign that they have, at last, begun to".

In respect to his bucket list, or perhaps his was a *fuckit* list, he could, and probably did, check off all the things he may have had on it. Life moves on. We left the legacy of a lifetime. Whatever happens now and, in the future, will be, as the announcer at the beginning of a horse race says, "in the hands of the starter". He called me a few months later to ask me to delete his number from my phone. I answered with, "WHO is this?"

COMMITTEE OF ONE

Now I'm responsible for many things that I never had to worry about before. Life has become a learning process. My car persisted in messaging me that I needed a maintenance check, so here I was, after having to make an appointment, in the Lexus lounge waiting for my car, which was undergoing its periodic checkup, one of the perks of marriage that I had to forego.

Sitting and waiting for your car is akin to waiting for medical results at a lab, especially when they tell you, upon leaving the car in their trusting hands, they will be doing diagnostic testing...whatever the hell that is. Every car being serviced has an owner waiting. They all appear to be anxious and uptight hoping their car technician doesn't find anything seriously wrong during their cars' routine maintenance.

You are told how long the inspection will take as you hand them your keys. The wait is two hours. Much like a surgeon, after performing a procedure on one of your loved ones, your personal *tech* advisor comes to find you in the waiting area and proceeds to speak to you in a hushed, solemn voice, lest anyone else become privy to this most enigmatic conversation. He tells you about the highly specialized and dedicated type of Lexus mechanics who will be taking personal responsibility for your car.

The other owners feign not listening, but they are, especially when they hear the word "transmission" or "drive train", which equates to "heart" or "internal bleeding" as far as severity of the problem goes.

As I sat in the lounge, opposite the Lexus café, I observed a young, attractive woman, waiting for her café latte, having to clean up puppy poop, dropped by her fluffy white Bichon Frise. I watched as she fussed over her pet. It was apparent she needed to give love, be loved, and be needed. Been there, done that. I had one St. Bernard, sundry fish, one turtle, one ring necked dove, two children, one husband, and conceivably, at one point, a partridge in a pear tree. That was yesterday, during a far different lifetime.

I love flying solo. Being married at 18, right after graduating high school, and divorced 56 years later, I had never lived by myself. For the first time in my life I feel liberated, and love my life. I'm doing anything and everything I want. The autonomy of going, doing, and being, without having to consult with another is vitalizing and stimulating. I never have to close the bathroom door.

Other than for resale, do I really need a bathroom door? I look forward to coming home from work, after being with people all day, and not having to see or talk to anyone, spending time with me.

This is a whole new wonderful way of life; an approach to living, and existing, that had never been considered, or even possible, before. Now, living my own life in the manner in which I choose, has become the norm. I have three plants: one teetering on the brink of extinction, and the other two, being in the succulent family, thrive on the acute neglect that they have become accustomed to. If and when any of them wither and die, they will not be replaced: just like me!

In my space I read, write, watch TV, or sit and watch the beautiful sunsets. My time is my own: I am the mistress of my universe. After almost six decades of having someone in my life and in my home, I indulge myself either with a big bowl of ice cream or a glass of wine while enjoying my happy place, on my balcony.

I am a perfect example that it's never too late, on the happiness scale of one to ten, to score a resounding ten.

YOU ARE NOT ALONE

You are not alone. You may be by yourself, but where are you really? Are you where your body is, or where your mind is? That question has stumped mankind for millennia. I sit on my balcony thinking of my life, the good, the bad, the sad, and the what-if's. Am I in those moments or in the present? Don't people talk of the spirit living on? Well, it's certainly not your body that's floating on the breeze. How often have we been touched by something we can't understand or see, a feeling, a hint of a breath, or a spider crawling up your pant leg, but can definitely feel?

You need to take the first step into your new zone, albeit, a giant one. That step is the only step you need to concern yourself with. It is amazing how your feet will follow each other after that initial stride. The more steps you take, the stronger you become. Divorce can be a good thing. In fact, it usually is a very good thing.

Marriage is such a strange phenomenon that both the married and the unmarried are, at times, unhappy for radically opposite reasons: one for being married, and one for not being married. Why stay with someone just because you dread living alone? There are very few things in life more miserable than being lonely in a marriage, other than your daughter's nose ring or maybe intestinal parasites... maybe.

Think about it, what will you miss most in a relationship that's gone bad? Will you miss the intimacy, that is now long gone, the need to touch and be touched, which may revolt you by now? Will you miss wanting to be there for another, to cook for and share mealtime which has probably not happened for months? Will you miss a companion who shares your love of the outdoors and enjoys long walks with you, or the closeness of a warm body lying next to you in bed? Perhaps you are missing opening your door and having that hello kiss? In most bad marriages the intimacy and frequency of these may already have soured, curdling like two-week-old milk, along with the relationship.

It's simple. Run, don't walk to your nearest animal shelter. What better friend than a dog? They love you and need you, unconditionally. If, in the off chance they try to run away, you can keep them on a leash. If that doesn't work for you, owning a parrot will fill the bill. In fact, don't you think that's a good name for your newest buddy, *Bill*? They offer companionship, are messy, need you to clean up after them, and say stupid things, probably not much different than your ex, or soon to be ex-spouse.

As I was writing this, it occurred to me, why not visit a shelter or a community for homeless people? Many of these men and women can be helped by compassion. Although they may be down and out, one should not count them out! The sadness and loneliness of these broken men and women might be turned around if someone took the time to help them understand themselves and help them understand that they can regain their place in society once they see there is hope, and someone who cares.

There are more treatments available now than ever before, and society is aware of their situations more than at any other time. A little kindness and encouragement can go a long way. Mom used to say, and how right she was, "Where there's life there's hope".

WHAT KIND OF PARTY?

You need to have a Pretty Party not a Pity Party. Don't just sit there reading. O.K., read another page or two...Now, get up and do something. Do something silly. Do something funny, something courageous, something bordering on what you once believed to be inane. Do something you never thought you would ever do.

Want to make a drastic change without changing a thing? Buy a wig; pick out an outrageous style or color. Buy some shocking clothes to go with your new look. Who knows, this could be the beginning of you fulfilling a long-ago fantasy. You may like this new look, and others' reactions to it, enough to make the change permanent. Dancing lessons, from tap to ballet, are available for every age. Are you still sitting there? For God's sake GET UP! Get started. If there is an unfulfilled desire in you, it's NEVER too late to *Do It.*

Brenda's thoughts: Explore the unknown Do you know that we don't know what we don't know? A day's excitement and acceleration have more value than weeks, months, even years of desolation.

Once you see, you cannot un-see. The same with memories, don't try to forget them; consider them building blocks of life. Let's eliminate keeping track of one's age by calendar years. How about zones? I am settled into the sixty-five- to eighty-year-old zone and have stopped counting years. Who could ever forget Satchel Paige's great line: "How old would you be if you didn't know how old you was?"

Going to work, I carry a book bag on my back in order to keep my hands free while walking. Then I was corrected, my book bag became my backpack, which I later called knapsack, when I was reminded of the song *Val de re, Val de ra*; the lyrics being, "*With my knapsack on my back*". It is now many bags, oops I mean packs later, and I updated the same old thing with a new name. It is now my jet pack. Let the others catch up to me!

A topic you must explore is your finances. Do you know how much you are worth? It's important to know exactly how much you have in holdings, and what and where you and your spouse have financial accounts. This includes any and all checking, bank, and stock accounts. Familiarize yourself with what the laws are in your state concerning comingled funds, marital funds, and/or individual accounts.

NEVER sign anything without reading and understanding what it is no matter how much your spouse will attempt to coerce you by saying it's nothing to trouble yourself about...because it is nothing to be concerned with. Anything you sign your name to is something to be concerned about.

If there is any doubt your relationship may be deteriorating, start doing your homework. There are some obvious signs that an end may be near. Learn them. If you find out your spouse has an account on Match.com ...be wary. If you take two vacations a year: you in June, and your spouse in October...be wary. If your spouse off-handedly asks how you feel about dating others...be wary.

If at all possible, don't leave home until you have your safeguards in place. Protect yourself; you may have only one chance at this and you want to leave a winner.

If you are, or have been saving your own funds, make certain you remember where you put them, and use a fire-proof metal box for that rainy day or your getaway. You don't want anything to happen, in case there's a fire or flood. As cynical as this may sound, take your soon-to-be not-beloved shopping. Buy that something valuable and wonderful you always wanted, as long as the other person is paying for it. When all is said and done, protect your dignity, self-respect, and financial security.

If you are the breadwinner, make sure you have your own money that's protected by **not** co-mingling funds, which then become marital assets. This includes any and all properties you own jointly. Each state may have variations of these laws. I strongly advise you to seek legal counsel and/ or professional accounting assistance before making that first move to your new zone.

Why am I writing, and why do I think I'm doing a good job of it? I think it's the compression of life. From March 1957 until he walked out of my life on August 26, twelve days before our fifty-sixth wedding anniversary, we shared a *"Long day's journey into night"*. Love found, love lost. I discovered why divorce is so expensive...it's worth it!

It's clean up time. What you do mentally, you do physically, and vice versa. The first thing I did was assess my situation when it was a foregone conclusion the party was over. I had to decide what I wanted to do for and with the rest of my life. Did I want to sit and pine away, "Oh, woe is me"? Well, the sitting part didn't sound so bad, but the depression part didn't seem to be an option I was ready to succumb to. Anything that easy can't be good for your health. Why should I sink when he had the opportunity to swim...with his substantial settlement that I worked for?

I started cleaning and clearing out his stuff, throwing it out, ripping up papers that no longer had any meaning, like old Hallmark cards, and giving things to charity. I found there is a very fine line between "cleaning", and "throwing away". Both achieve the same results, more space and less clutter in my head as well as my condo! I did not give any of his things to anyone I knew. No way did I want to see someone in something he once owned.

I felt the need for some emotional intervention. I joined two Reiki circles and allowed myself to garner the support these groups gave to me, and others. I felt the need to be there. One day the need was not there and letting go happened effortlessly. It seemed it was nature's way of saying, *been there, done that*, now move on.

AUTO PAY

Delving into virgin territory and attempting to make bill-paying as effortless as possible, I endeavored to put as many accounts as I could on "Auto-Pay", making for fewer things I would have to think about, or remember. I looked at this task as being highly technical and used excuse after excuse to delay the execution of this modern convenience.

For all of my married life, FLOML was my autopay. When I ran out of excuses, and forced myself, it would take at least three phone calls to complete each account that I wanted to put on auto pay. I was at my wits end when I would call and attempt to figure out what was going on.

Being the fifth caller, and after twenty minutes of waiting, I was answered by a breathy, sexy voice.

"This is Van-Ella. Welcome to Havaheart Service Company. How may I assist you today?"

I tell her and she continues, "How are you today?"

I think for a few seconds. *Is she serious? Could she honestly care how I feel today? Is it even today in India?* Should I succumb to Van-Ella's kind voice? *Should I tell her that I am past the breaking point, and the stress is killing me? That my body is breaking down with shooting pains here, spasms there, sciatica, and how can I forget my shortness of breath? I pause a few seconds grasping the consequences of an honest answer.*

"Fine," I reply. "Awesome," she replied.

After requesting my name, Van-Ella asks, "May I call you Brenda?"

Who the fuck cares? I think. Wait, did I say that aloud? Please God say "no!"

"Yes," I answer, in order to move the conversation along. I am also aware of the other callers, stacked up like airplanes in the wild blue yonder, waiting for their turn to land.

She asks me a myriad of questions, to which I have the answers, but there is always at least one question where the answer eludes me.

I never went on the computer to pay anything. One of his responsibilities was paying the bills. That task always seemed so daunting to me. Once upon a time, more than fifty years ago, I opened a bill and asked why it was so high. He said to me ruefully, "If you're not going to pay them, don't open them". Not only did I never open another bill, but I never picked up the mail, and now, one year after becoming a solo act, I have to remind myself to go to the mailroom at least once a week.

At that time, his response was music to my ears. Who wanted to deal with the scary complexities of managing banking, balancing checkbooks, and paying bills? All those numbers spooked me.

But I digress. I never understood and did not know the code needed to be broken in order to reach the Land of Oz, the Holy Land...the land of autopay. Once the secret code to the land of acceptance was discovered, a fresh new world of open space and a brightly shining sun on an idyllic landscape materialized. I had a chance of reaching Nirvana. That's it! I'll tackle this new world as though it was a board game. I'll call it *Cyberspace Heaven.*

Once you completed the password and username hurdles, you were required to successfully remember at least two of the following:

1. Your dogs' name: *Coffee*
2. Your favorite cartoon character, even if you don't have one: *Tweety Bird.*
3. The year your mother went to her high school prom: *Huh?*
4. The date of your first sexual encounter: *That one was easy, my wedding night.*
5. And lastly, your favorite Broadway play, even if you never saw one: *Cats.*

After completing this, cyber-sky was the limit as to what lay ahead ... or so I thought.

After giving the account info and explaining why the name on the account needed to be changed, I began to achieve a modicum of success. It's gotta be easier to get into the White House or a South Beach Club.

Whether on their website typing in answers, or speaking to a representative, there was always one question for which I had no answer. I had climbed the ladder of the giant slide to the top only to find myself slipping all the way to the bottom, never reaching the goal of Nirvana and the heavenly gates of the Internet, based solely on the fact that I was unaware of my grandfather's mother's maiden name. I have one word for all of this...Fuck!

Little did I know that complete happiness and lightness of mind and body could be reached only by knowing the code, made up of a password and a username, which must consist of at least eight letters, a numeric symbol (why can't they just say number?), and an additional non-numeric symbol? When was the "pound sign" replaced by "hashtag" and what the hell is a "hashtag"? How had it morphed from tic-tac-toe to pound sign, to hashtag, when in actuality there was no known usage of the symbol before the mid 60's, when Bell Labs dubbed it the "octothorpe"?

We talk about going into outer space, we live in inner space, but where is cyberspace? Is it a place you send your mind to, the way you send your kids to summer camp? Your mind and your words are all that's necessary to become a member in good standing and acceptance to this magical place. Is there a theme park called cyberspace at Disney World?

I am answering Van-Ella's questions, or, I am on their web site, filling in the blanks. If your entry is wrong, red print pops up and you need to go back and start over. Only dots or star symbols pop up on a line when you put in your secret code, so you have no way of knowing where you went wrong. Two more tries and if you haven't figured it out . . . it's *game over.*

What should be said by the faceless voice rather than, "to whom do I have the pleasure of speaking?" is, "Welcome. Make sure your seatbelt is buckled and securely fastened because you are entering cyberspace, which will be the trip of a lifetime. Your experience is going to be the best or worst one of your life and will either be the smoothest or the bumpiest ride you can possibly imagine."

The coup de gras happens when you are on their website, push all the right keys, and you're feeling pretty smug and relieved about getting to the end. But alas, at that point, one of two things happens: either you get disconnected, or words pop up telling you that you have been on too long and it shuts off.

"Good-bye".

The connection has timed out.

Try again

THINGS THAT START AND END WITH D*

After an incredibly long, and oft times fun run, the party ended, and not with a bang or any teary good-byes. I must move on and adjust to the void and deal with no longer having my needs met by another.

I must take that one giant step into the chasm called the future, and I will... and furthermore, to quote Gloria Gaynor, "I will survive". Will I miss what will be no longer a part of my life, like falling asleep to the sound of his voice? Will I miss him no longer being there to comfort me late at night? Perhaps...or perhaps not, comfort can be achieved in so many other ways.

I know it is said that time heals all wounds, and most absences. I am hoping that is true. Everything comes to an end and I must adjust and move on or I will stagnate, like standing water, and get lost in the past. I will always celebrate what I had while it lasted, some tears, some disappointments, but a lot of laughs. We went through a great deal together. We were together for so long, some would say almost a lifetime.

Today is the first day, a fresh beginning, one with the past left behind. Those fond and not so fond memories are mine to have and to hold. It is the dawning of new horizons. I will throw my knapsack, err, jetpack, on my back and set out to seek fresh possibilities, I will travel off the beaten path into that unknown, albeit exciting territory called the future.

I will have the freedom to roam the world and not have to consider who or what I am missing. No longer will I, or must I, think, "Will he be in good mood? Will he make me laugh? Who will be with him? Will I be jealous of the people he chooses to share with me?" His humor and a glass of Chablis helped wash away the travails of the day.

When I was not able to be with him, did I want to know what I missed? Ahhh, to record or not to record. You were there when I needed you. You were there when I wanted you and it was fun while it lasted. Thank you and goodbye David Letterman, you, I will miss.

In my mind and heart, today the 21st of May 2015, marked the end of an era. After thirty-three years, David Letterman had his last show. Sadly, the show is no longer, it's over; so, onward and upward. There will be life without David Letterman, just as there was life after Jack Paar, Johnny Carson, and Jay Leno.

We need to enter into a new zone of entertainment and learn to live Letterman-less, and we will. On this same, momentous day our divorce became final in the courts or so I believed. Letterman retired. FLOML and I can celebrate that we lasted 23 more years than he did.

Lots of laughter lots of tears,
All through our being together for so many years.
We had some laughs we had some tears But through it all we survived 56 years.
Some years were good and some years were bad And some years we wished we never had.

The conclusion of this story is that Brett, my Brilliant Barrister (BBB) called me at 10 a.m. to tell me the deed was done; FLOML's attorney had gone to court and signed off. The divorce papers were now official. It was over. Yay! I was now a single woman. BBB and I then went on to discuss topical events.

He's writing a book, and I, my primer. I went about my business, not giving any thought to my new status: divorced, detached, determined, or whatever. At 3:30 p.m. I received another call from BBB which snatched the joyful conclusion right out of my reality. He was calling to inform me that his lawyer didn't go to court, due to a question concerning a withdrawal I made from my IRA Account that the incompetent idiot could have resolved with a thirty second phone call to BBB.

I had a meltdown, regurgitating all the bitterness and frustrations that I felt from having to give so much of my retirement funds, which was especially painful due to the fact that he didn't earn any of it. If you don't think that it's a man's world, in a man's club, in a man's court of fuckin' law, think again.

Now, it was back to the drawing board and the bank, for more bickering, and, of course, costing more bucks. This was illustrated most succinctly when I received this note from the law office: *As your attorney, it is my duty to inform you that it is not important that you understand what I am doing, or why you are paying me so much money. What is important is that you continue to do so.* It seems to me that in order to succeed in law, it is often necessary to rise above your principles. The deed was done July 15, 2015. Finally!

*David, Divorced, Delayed.

NOBODY CAN SEE PAIN

I love it when someone bestows their saddest, "I feel your pain" face. No one really does, you know. They want you to think they do...but they don't, they can't. The next time someone says, "I feel your pain," just reach out and jab them with a sharpened pencil, and somberly tell them, "OK, now I believe you."

Each and every person's emotions and stories are unique. Sure, there are many similarities, but like fingerprints, no two tales are exactly alike. Make a gray day a blissful day. Think of it as war games. This strategy confuses your enemies, and that's the way you want it.

When you are going through a life changing trauma such as divorce or separation, people close to you are expecting, and even looking forward to hearing your depressing, heartbreaking story. Why wouldn't they? Most will revel in it, it will make their day, and their lives seem that much better. That's just how most people are.

One person's misfortunes are but a source of entertainment and inspiration to others. Don't give them what they want. Give them what you want, a happy story. Leave them slack-jawed and disappointed. Why set yourself up to be someone else's lunch conversation? Bad overrides glad in most persons' conversational interests, just like TV newscasts.

Don't give your friends food for thought as they are crunching and munching on their salads. Let them find someone else's misery to chew on. You don't have to descend to the level of despair your friends expect.

Drive them crazy. Does anyone really like a happy divorcee? Make them question what secret you may be hiding. Make them speculate, "What the hell is she so happy about, what am I missing here? Why can't I be that happy?"

Put on a smile. Your friends and enemies alike will be confused with your happy face. They will wonder what they have overlooked. You no longer fit their stereotype. It will drive them crazy.

When you decide to play the part, you will become the role that you play. Rise and fly above theirs, and your own expectations. Think positive and stay positive. How you appear to others will carry over to your own self-image. Begin to believe and convince yourself of the positive aspects of your situation, and what may lie ahead, and you will achieve a happiness level far greater than your friends will expect, or even demand.

Don't think you know who your enemies are. In a divorce situation your closest friend may turn out to be somebody you should not have trusted, but enough about them. Ditch them like an old moth-eaten suit. You may initially experience confusion, sadness, emptiness, despair, and a feeling of, *where do I go from here?* You're going to get through it because if you don't, the other team wins. This is a story of you putting on those tap shoes and dancing happily into the sunset. Have you ever seen an un-happy tap dancer?

The sooner you face the reality that you now count for something, and you are now someone new, the more effortlessly and comfortably you can move ahead and make the necessary transitions. "Said and done" is exactly that, "Said and done". There is no taking back the spoken word; it's out there, just like an e-mail or a naked picture on the web.

Your earliest feelings may be of dejection, rejection, confusion, despair, and "should I go on?" Why? Will any of those thoughts make you feel any better? Will they move you forward? Absolutely not! Get up, get out, and move on! You have a life to live. You can read this later. The words will still be on the pages just the way you left them. You are in for the time of your life. Fasten your seatbelt, this ride's in motion.

"Sometimes good things fall apart so better things can fall together."

—Marilyn Monroe

BECOME THE 'I SHALL' SEEKER

L ife, regardless of your age, begins as soon as your eyes open in the morning. You must do SOMETHING. You shall talk to your frienemies. Don't be shy to ask if they know of something that you don't. You shall talk to men or women who are going through similar ordeals as you. Most of what I write about is also fitting for widows and widowers who think life was about being part of a twosome. There are clubs and organizations covering almost any interest or life experience.

This information is available for viewing whenever you are. All you have to do is turn on your computer and Google the magic words of what interests you, and your zip code, to introduce you to a new life. If you can't find something that piques your interest, even for a short time, you may not be making enough of an effort.

In my case, a friend suggested I enroll in a writing class. I said, "No". She continued to encourage me until I happened upon a writing group through a *Meet-up* website. That free thinking group helped open up whatever was locked away in the recesses of my brain, waiting to finally explode out of its shell. You cannot make up for lost time, but as the expression goes, "Better late than never."

Don't be a whiner, be a winner. You win when you don't succumb to your melancholia. When was the last time you visited your public library?

Do you know they have a variety of excellent programs and events that may peak your interest, ranging from apple picking to Zumba, from A to Z. You will never know until you try it. Everything is not for everyone, but there is something for everyone. It's easy to go on and on about this scavenger hunt of finding satisfaction in life. The opportunities are endless; find that something that is perfect for you.

Remember, when you are a *party of one,* when you decide to change course, you can. The only thing stopping you, is you. Go shopping or at least *get thee to a mall.* Take a seat, have a café or a carafe of wine and enjoy the people parade. It's mesmerizing.

Before you know it, you will be making up stories about the people passing by, and you will lose yourself in these stories. You have got to let go! Before you know it, you have taken a bad time, and a sad time, and turned it into a glad time.

Every day is a new adventure. Sitting and moping are easy to succumb to. That's NOT fine, nor healthy. Do something positive with this melancholia. Buy yourself a sweatshirt for your next workout and personalize it by having 'QUITTER' printed on it.

"No way," you say? Great! Now that I have your attention you have just made a giant step towards liberation. I didn't think quitting is your thing.

Enjoy yourself, you will either feel better or feel worse. One thing's for sure, you won't stay the same. On that note, some days you may want to lie around, watch TV re-runs, eat junk food, fall asleep, wake up, eat ice cream and potato chips, and then start all over again. Do it! By the next day you will have had enough. Give in to yourself without guilt and then get over it, pick yourself up, and get on with your life.

Many communities nowadays have social functions for older people: dancing, cards, exercise classes, current events. I don't have to spell them all out for you. Find out for yourself, it's as easy as picking up a newspaper or Googling clubs and events and seeing what's available. Computers are not your thing . . how do you know? Take a beginner's course before you say it's not for you. The one thing you need to know is that you must get yourself up and out. They are not coming to you, although they may come *for you*, and that you do not want!

Today is not the day of the pity party but it is for the pretty party. Start by going shopping in your closet, *Hey! Do you see a new garment tag hanging on that jacket? Wow, you forgot you bought it!* Try it on, not bad, build your day's ensemble around your new item. Introduce your new jacket and yourself to your new day ... Today.

WHERE DO YOU GO FROM HERE?

You are newly single. Where do you go from here? The simple answer is, anywhere you want. Carry on with your job, if you have one; carry on with your next-door neighbor, if you're not already. Staying with your job helps to keep your head and body together. Take this opportunity to make new acquaintances, and/or renew old friendships and family ties.

Carrying on with your next-door neighbor could get messy, so I recommend someone not so geographically available. Visit dating web sites, and of course, partake in all of the social Medias. You will come to love the lack of restrictions now placed on going, doing, and being, without having to deal with another's opinion, suggestion, or advice that once stymied you. You now make all the rules.

At this juncture of my life, using the happiness scale of one to ten, I give myself a resounding ten.

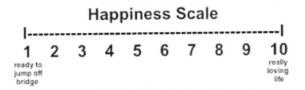

Everything is subject to change, and, at my age, I have become a confirmed realist, which means that now, I am concerned with facts, practicality, the literal truth, and most importantly, what is best for me. Let us not forget what the great H. L. Menken said about idealists: "An idealist is one who, on noticing that roses smell better than a cabbage, concludes that it will also make a better soup". Keep it real! The difference between live, and lie is the 'V', V for victory. When you live with yourself, there are no more lies. You may not recognize it, but you are victorious and that is why you are who you are, and why you are where you are.

Expect the unexpected. Make your home look more like, 'YOU live here' rather than, 'WE live here'. That is your new reality, as well as your new identity. My condo is beginning to look like either an artist or writer resides in its homey confines.

In addition to having papers all over the place for the documents I needed for my divorce, I found old letters and articles that I had written in my other life, looking to see if they could be recycled and slightly altered in order to reflect the 21st-century, as well as my continually changing outlook on what it is to be alive, instead of just existing. What a mess! But who cares! My home is my castle, in which there is but one Queen...and that is me.

I do not pamper myself like many other women, but everyone needs something that brings them pleasure, something that makes them feel good about being alive. For me, it's having a personal assistant. They are no more costly than manicures, pedicures, massages, and facials.

Historically, I never read directions or instructions for anything new, like a computer, an iPhone, popcorn popper, or even an iron. I once failed to heed the warning about not ironing your clothes while wearing them, since I did and I was. My modus operandi has become when in doubt, call on a good friend, return the item, or hire an assistant, even a very part time one. Whatever floats your boat; you need to have and enjoy one luxury you should not deny yourself.

When I joined a writing group, encouraged by Terry, my friend since elementary school, she assured me that the writing would be a game changer, and boy, was she spot-on! I could feel emotional weight leaving my very being, like an innocent verdict after a lengthy trial, when I began to write. The most important aspect is the "Lets' Do" facet, which I am doing' with the hope that you, my readers will follow suit and also can, and will "Do It!"

The more I wrote, the more the floodgates of thoughts opened. I felt like a bursting dam. I found it challenging to stay on target, i.e., this primer.

I have the attention span of a six-year-old, un-medicated child. Not like today's kids who are either on Prozac, the computer, or a combo of electronics and prescribed tranquilizing drugs, which attempt to keep them calm and focused...much like mute zombies. My aphrodisiac is life and chocolate! Oh yes, and an occasional glass or two of wine. I am a drug free zone. I must be in control of my mind and my body.

My entry into the world of real estate more than forty years ago was a stopgap, until I could find something I really wanted to do. Well, that didn't happen, until now, over four decades later. I want to be a writer. Who would've ever *thunk* it? If it can happen for me, it can happen for you! Living with conflict seems to be my fuel of choice for maintaining my energy level.

New conflicts surround me as I sit in front of my computer having meltdown after meltdown trying to make sense of such things as marital finances. "Big deal", you are thinking, but for me it is a big deal. I just turned seventy-five, and for the first time in my life I am faced with economics 101-through whatever degree one gets in the school of real-life finance.

At my age what I expected to happen hasn't happened, so far: cancer, heart disease, diabetes, broken hips, replaced knees, and other old age symptoms requiring medical attention. With a trim here and a shot there I am managing to hold off the typical old lady look, at least for now.

The bills that come in the mail, boldly stating *Final Notice,* or *Dated Material.* What is the real deal? I can't figure out some of them, even though most of the ones that seem important, like Florida Power and Light, are now on auto pay, which seems to be working, as my lights have not yet been turned off. In addition, on the rare times I use my stove, it still heats up.

What about that daunting letter stating that I missed my dental appointment? Did I really make that appointment for a cleaning, or did they send me that letter so I would think I made one? No, upon making that call I learned it was their way of cajoling you into making one before your teeth fall out.

I liken myself to a rupturing volcano, with all the external pressures pushing in on my outlet to the world, causing an eruption. In this scenario, instead of lava flowing, it's about words and ideas surging and oozing out of my newly awakened brain. My best friends are now a blank piece of paper or a new document in WORD. I am loading it up with my new associates, my black and white characters, my words.

One of the most important "Must Do's" for the "Let's Do" audience is to have your Pity Party, and then for God's sake, and your own best interests, move on. As my friend's mother always says about life's pitfalls, "Get over it!" Finish this sentence, "Wallowing in the past is good for me because..." I bet you can't think of one viable reason, since there isn't one. Don't waste your valuable time on something you can do absolutely nothing about, and that includes the past.

Your options are now limited only by your own parameters. You need to choose one that's just right for you. Let's start. Options and goals are like buying a coat. You try it on, it looks fantastic, and the color is great. Everything about it is good, except that it doesn't feel right, it's tight when you move your arms across your chest. If it doesn't fit, take it off, forget about it, and move on to the next coat, or even the next rack. Don't buy into or become anything that is uncomfortable. It's not how it looks, it's how it feels.

Cast it away, run, don't walk to your nearest exit. Move on... onward and upward. This is all about YOU, all about NOW. This is all about TODAY and TOMORROW and the rest of your life.

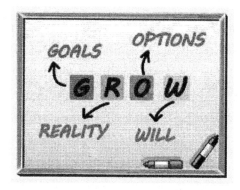

JUST SAY NO

Don't be color blind. Every day, pick out a color, any color. If it's red, look for anything and everything that is, or has red on it. This is easy, fun and most importantly, good for your mind.

Your awareness of noticing and observing will be heightened by focusing on one thing, the target that you choose, which in this case, is the color red. You will see your surroundings in a completely different and more vivid way. What was or appeared to be commonplace and ho-hum will take on a whole new dimension. Get your mind off the negative and focus on the positive. You can do it!

If you feel a need to seek professional support to put you and your mind on the right track, I recommend a therapy called "Accelerated Resolution Therapy" (A.R.T.), founded by Laney Rosenzweig, who happens to be my cousin. (www.artworksnow.com) Regardless of my relationship, this therapy can fix your problem in as little as one session. It can, and will, ease your anxiety, allowing you to focus on positive, not negative matters.

One of the most important, life-altering skills you can achieve is knowing how to say "no" to persons who request things that neither enthuse nor support you, or in simple terms, you just do not want to do! Your friends and family will try to take advantage of you, thinking that "She's/He's alone, I'm sure they won't mind running an errand, babysitting, senior sitting, etc." If you can positively say this is what YOU want, of course, go for it, say "yes", otherwise you must learn to say "no". If need be, stand in front of a mirror, check your stance and practice until you are convincing to yourself.

Many people say "No" but their body language is saying, "Well..., maybe". Most people don't just say "no". Instead they vacillate, and say something like, "Any other time ...", or "I would but..." which gives the questioner an open ended opportunity to try again. They will persist with "How about Thursday?", or "Well, I'll pick you up if it's too far for you to drive." If they think there is even a small flicker of doubt in your persistence to decline an invitation to go or do something, demand of the asker, "What part of 'no' don't you understand?

Say "No," without explanation, or offer up an answer with a comparable response that leaves little doubt as to your meaning, and leaves no room for an alternative, such as "I can't this time," or "sorry, not today," or "that does not work for me, I'll call you if things change."

Be firm, be clear, understand no excuses are necessary, and prioritize your limits and abilities to accomplish things that you want to do. Remember, if something is less important than what you have to give up to undertake it, be assertive and just say "NO!"

As time goes by, it will become easier, and the requests will stop. Meet your own needs before those of others and stop trying to please everyone. Remember, you are in charge of what you allow into your life.

On the other hand, if you are looking to supplement your income, these requests can turn into money making opportunities. Qualified baby, house, or senior sitters, can be a lucrative earning opportunity, earning you a minimum of $12.00 an hour. Go for it, it will be money well-earned and good for your head and your pocketbook.

THINGS TO KNOW AND HEED WHEN "TIL DEATH DO US PART" ISN'T ATTAINED

There will almost always be alimony.

While younger couples may have temporary alimony (now defined as: the high cost of leaving) agreements that provide financial support for their ex, often last only long enough for lower earning spouses to get back on their feet, it's a different situation for those exiting long-term marriages.

In New York, for example, the court will generally give alimony for life. What's customary for alimony can vary, but legal experts say senior couples can expect it to play some role in their divorce proceedings.

If they're working, they're going to pay some alimony, and if they are not working, such as in FLOML's case, they will receive an undeserved, as well as unearned, abundance of remuneration from the one party that has been working, as in my situation, my tail off for over 40 years.

Alimony is a system by which, when two people make a mistake, one of them keeps paying for it.

Your retirement money is about to be cut in half, or more.

It doesn't matter if one spouse was considered at-fault for the divorce, most attorneys say retirement funds and other assets are likely to be split evenly. (Ahh, if only this were true). What looked like a lot of money to live on in your senior years doesn't look like much when cut in half.

Some spouses may offer more of their pension to avoid making alimony payments, however, it may not be a person's best interest to accept a deal that would trade tax-favored investments for potentially taxable income. Or, in one case, which I happen to be quite familiar with, my case, FLOML received seventy five percent of the retirement funds. I'm guessing the judge liked him best.

If you keep the house, there will be a trade-off.

Many women balk at giving up their marital residence. While it can be an emotional decision to give up a longtime home, it may be one that makes the most financial sense, particularly when courts often split assets evenly. If you take the house, it has a value, in which case your husband is going to get something in his column to balance that out.

That something could be a greater share of a pension or a smaller alimony obligation. Either way, keeping the house and giving up retirement savings or cash payments could put a person in a bind. Houses come with property taxes, maintenance expenses and other costs that can stretch already meager financial resources. Since you are starting fresh, this could be the best time to sell your family home, take the profit and re-establish yourself in a bachelor-style home, condo, or adult community where you can live in your own home and enjoy all the activities available in your new neighborhood.

Your kids may be older, but they might still be a factor.

Divorce can be a hard transition at any stage. The silver lining of senior divorce is that it's not going to have the same gut-wrenching kid issues that younger couples have. In most elder divorces, child support and visitation orders are not a concern. However, that doesn't mean adult children aren't a consideration in the divorce proceedings.

Research has shown that most adult children are shocked when they learn their parents are divorcing – even if the children knew their parents' marriage had been rocky for years. That shock is followed by a lingering disbelief, and a deep and abiding sense of loss.

It's not unusual for parents to provide financial support for adult children, and while adult children may want this support to continue, it's not something typically written into a divorce agreement unless a child has a disability or is in school. You simply can't obligate someone to pay a third party. The same applies to couples who may be supporting elderly parents.

As a result, some divorcees may end up in the difficult position of having to decide whether to use their diminished savings or income to continue this support. Finally, adult children may react emotionally to their parents' divorce so don't burden your children with your dirty laundry or force them to take sides. There is no reason to over-share if everyone seems to be adjusting appropriately, but parents shouldn't have to keep the reasons behind the divorce a secret. They should disclose only if it brings resolution and is needed to help offspring make sense of what's happening.

Bitterness benefits no one, but don't be your ex's best buddy.

Emotions run high during a divorce, but experts say to try to keep conversations neutral.

It doesn't matter how old you are, be as amicable as possible. There is no benefit in having a contentious divorce. Being amicable isn't the same as being an open book. Sharing information such as future plans, favorite possessions, or desired assets will give a spouse considerable negotiating power during divorce proceedings. Be polite, be civil, but keep it to yourself, and above all keep it businesslike.

After the divorce is final you can walk away saying, been there, done that, GOODBYE. I don't understand divorced partners boasting how they are good friends. Your ex asking to be friends after a divorce is sort of like kidnappers asking to keep in touch after letting you go. So, hell no! If I liked him well enough to be his friend, wouldn't we still be married?

when your ex says:
"you'll never find anyone like me"
reply with:
"that's the point"

Never start dating before your divorce is final.

Getting a divorce can have an impact on relationships beyond the marriage. It can polarize friends and leave some ex-spouses feeling alone and defensive. It's important, as a senior person, when you get a divorce, to not let yourself be isolated. Possible outlets for social interaction could be community events, volunteer activities or even hitting the campaign trail for your favorite candidate in the next election.

However, newly single seniors shouldn't make the mistake of squandering their blank slate and jumping into a new relationship too quickly. Give yourself a chance, you may find that you are your best company. Dating before your divorce is final never makes things better. It can upset children, anger the soon-to-be ex-spouse, and add time and money to the proceedings.

Just for the record, dating while still married can be a major cause of divorce. Most importantly, think with your head and not your heart. Stay away from rebound romance. Once the bloom is off the rose, you may scratch your head and say, "What the hell did I do"? Don't find yourself in the same type of a relationship you just divorced.

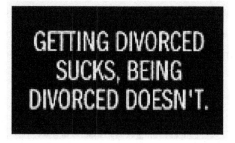

GETTING DIVORCED SUCKS, BEING DIVORCED DOESN'T.

Get a prenuptial agreement for the second time around.

With re-marriages being more likely to end in divorce than first marriages, family law experts advise anyone considering another union to get a prenuptial agreement. Without one, a second divorce can take retirement savings that have already been split once and divide them even further. Do the math, and then think real hard about that next marriage. Don't pay to play.

If there are any doubts, be prepared.

If you feel that you are not going to make it to the finish line aka, 'til death do you part,' do as much damage control as you can before firing off the first salvo of the conflict that will be. The primary step in ending your marriage should be having a confidential, free of charge, meeting with an attorney, or two, in the state where you will be filing. Double check what he/she tells you by doing your own research.

As much as possible, shield your financial assets, protect them. Check with your CPA. Ignorance of the laws in your state will cost you money, as a matter of fact, ignorance, by itself, is a primary cause of wasting money. To help you out even further, there is even a new divorce magazine on the market. The subscription is free, but if you want to end it, it's $2500.00 a month.

Some of the warning signs I missed, when I look back, were so obvious.

Change in personality. When he had his first liaison, with his lady friend, he was warm, romantic, and solicitous to me. Fast forward to before he left for the last time...he was critical and distant. Highly noticeable personality changes are a warning sign that sudden transformations in behavior can be a game changer in your own life.

If you recognize your relationship is less than solid and beginning to crumble, run, don't walk to your nearest attorney or financial advisor and find out how best to protect your interests, as well as assets. This is just in case the smoke you see is only the beginning, and as we know, where's there's smoke, there's fire.

PILLOW TALK...AND INSPIRATIONS

Dear reader, if perchance you picked up this book thinking that it would be a bit of pity patter, and you were looking to commiserate with the writer and nod your head in agreement because you felt that life had dealt you a regretful, losing hand, put the book down...now!. This is not the book for you.

This is not about being mad or sad; it's about going forward and being glad. It is about taking advantage of a situation that has befallen you and given you the power to reposition yourself into a life of your own choosing. I have no doubts that many of you have pictured that scenario many times in your past.

Once upon a time, in a life far away, or those times when I was restless and unable to sleep, and if laziness did not rear its ugly head, I would quietly get out of bed, careful not to awaken FLOML, and head for another room to write. At that time, I was an insomniac. I had such a serious case that when I fell asleep, I dreamt I was awake.

In that former life I did not have the self-confidence or desire to share my writings and thoughts with others, they were mine, and only mine. I would fold the papers and stow them away in secretive places. So very secret, that I forgot where I put them. We moved many times, and through our twenty or so relocations, those thoughts and papers disappeared and were lost along with broken memories, thanks to local movers and my own carelessness.

In 2001, my granddaughter, Abigail, was born. She was the inspiration I needed, and I began keeping travel journals. As I traversed the world, I began sending "Dear Abbey" chronicles of my experiences and visits to far-away places.

In more recent times, during the quiet, darkest hours of the night, I once again resorted to tapping away on my computer, away from the bedroom.

In my early days of electronic story writing, I would reach the end of what I thought was a well thought out narrative, only to look up and see a blank screen. I would stare vacantly at the bare screen and wonder where my thoughts had gone. I never found out, and never started over.

As we all know, life is forever in flux. Now that no one else shares my bed, I sleep with my iPhone at my side. I find this not only convenient, but comforting, as so many times I wake up thinking about anything and everything.

One night an awareness lit up in my mind: if I dictated those random and frequent thoughts into my i-Phone's "voice memo" notes app, I would be able to get things off my chest and empty my brain of those slumber-stealing thoughts right then and there. This allowed me to hold on to the inspirations and ideas that previously would have been lost forever, much like my early writings.

Many times, I find myself laughing...laughing out loud. I think of something that strikes me funny and who cares there's no one or no audience to share it with, because humor is not universal and, anyways, I think I am funny. I make myself laugh. It's a wonderful gift to have the power to amuse yourself.

Imparting my thoughts to my iPhone is akin to waking up because of a need to go to the bathroom. You really don't want to get up and go, and you think you can trick your mind and body into thinking you don't have to go, but alas, you become aware of the consequences if you don't get up, and just do it. So, you see, emptying my brain is like emptying my bladder. It is something I am compelled to do.

The sooner I do it, the quicker I can get back to sleep. The longer I prolong the inevitable, the less time there is for quality rest, and my thoughts fade away like the color in over-washed jeans. I must, therefore, get up. It has occurred to me that if I drink water before bedtime, I'll have to get up in the middle of the night to "go". But if I don't take that drink, I'll get up in the middle of the night because I'm thirsty. So, it looks like I'm going to get up anyway. I have learned to make good use of that time.

I dictate with the lights off, lying in bed. My phone has not yet learned to completely recognize my voice. I find this difficult to comprehend, as I have only one voice, and I am the solitary entity who talks to my phone. It should know me by now. Nevertheless, invariably the next morning, I check to see what I said during the night and some of the words I see or hear are not in my vocabulary, nor do some of them even exist in the Official Scrabble Dictionary.

After emptying my bladder, er, I mean, my brain, I fall back asleep assured that I do not have to worry about remembering what was on my mind, it was saved. I no longer had to think about it. It was written and notated so that I could bring it up whenever I wanted. I didn't lose it, which up until my learning that I could save everything I said on my phone, was a near impossibility.

I now sleep like a hibernating bear. I have accepted the fact that my phone is still in a learning process, but in due time we shall become i-Friends. Basically, what I have learned is that I can turn last night's random, unconnected thoughts and dreams into reality, as I laugh myself to sleep.

THE JOYS AND PERKS OF AGING

M emo to readers: Don't act old, and for God's sake park in-between the lines, not on them! If you are a slow driver, stay to the right, again, not on the line, but to the left of it. If you find driving home, after being out at night has lost its panache, then what is it you can't do during the day that you think you must do at night? Above all stay safe and try not to kill others.

Society has branded persons past a certain age senior citizens because of a chronological age, of let's say sixty. Once you hit this number, you are entitled to a number of perks. Take advantage of them. Some of these consist of discounts at Mac Donald's (for coffee), cut-rate admission tickets to most theaters, and numerous and varied shows that are discounted for students and seniors. Hmmm, do you think they give you an additional discount if you are both?

You know you are getting old, when you visit your child's home, and there on the cocktail table is his or her latest copy of the *AARP Magazine*. Other perks are assigned seats for the handicapped and/or seniors on trains and busses, and at waiting areas like the airport. Before you leave home, go to your computer and see what discounts are available to you for your days' outing. You may be surprised. When in doubt, "ASK." Mom always said, "If you don't ask, you don't get."

Some other positive perks of becoming a senior citizen, which most people don't even think of, are that kidnappers are not very interested in you, no one expects you to run anymore, there is nothing left to learn the hard way, and you no longer try to hold your stomach in, no matter who walks into the room. Perks abound for the newly aged.

One of the things many people are not aware of, in or out of the senior zone, are samples, especially pharmaceutical prescriptions. Everyone who goes to the doctor leaves the office with two things: a prescription, and a return appointment. Don't be intimidated to asking the doctor, doctor's assistant, or nurse for samples. Sometimes they say "Yes" and will give you enough to see if the prescription actually is making a difference for your ailments. Some simply refuse.

I have been given samples of prescribed medications that had adverse effects on me. By allowing me to have that sample, it saved me countless hundreds of dollars. I have personally seen, soon to be, or already expired samples in dumpsters behind medical centers. When in doubt, ask for no more than half the amount on the prescription which will still save you money and you won't feel silly as you throw out all the meds that didn't work. Regardless, if you do or do not have prescription insurance coverage, eventually someone is paying for all this waste. And we know, that in the end, it's us.

Are you aware that in today's consumer market, prescribed drugs, even if they are not opened, cannot be returned? These are the only purchased products that cannot be returned because they don't work. Even car companies let you test drive a car before you commit to purchasing it. With an impressive lobby in Washington, D.C. the big Pharmas are running and ruining society. Again, who gets hit the hardest is the ever shrinking middle-class.

You can't please everyone. As long as we are on the subject of products and returns: if you are not completely satisfied you got your money's worth from reading this primer, that you didn't get at least one hint, tip or any words of encouragement I will (reluctantly) with your sales receipt, refund your money, plus the cost of sending it back to me. Email me your contact info and I will send you shipping instructions.

Shh, let's not tell the "label" makers that at this age we feel better, have more energy, more enthusiasm, more joie de vie, than we did 20 years earlier. Our eyes probably won't get any worse, things we buy now won't wear out, and our supply of brain cells is finally down to a manageable size.

We are spending money on keeping ourselves as young as we feel, and we are out in the world living it up. Living by oneself is liberating. Not having to watch your every word, thought, and doing for the sake of another is a plus, and reduces stress. So, be who you are and say whatever you want, because those who matter don't mind, and those who mind ... don't matter.

Doing laundry for one, washing dishes, and watching TV as loud or soft as you want are even more perks of living as one. You may add to this list of what makes you happy once you decide you have had enough.

Live stress-less. Stress is when you wake up screaming and realize you haven't fallen asleep yet. Not being a doctor, I can't give medical advice, but everyone knows stress kills. It's been said stress is the number one health problem in the industrialized world as it can raise your blood pressure. High anxiety raises all forms of negative reactions in your system, bringing you down, and ultimately, depressing you.

Dodge that bullet. You must get rid of the tensions in your life that are bad for your health. That may include going out on your own. Get your *pins* in order. You and you alone must learn how to protect your well-being and analyze what's good for you. What time is it now? Altogether now, shout out, **This is 'ME' time.**

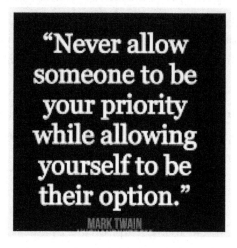

> **"Never allow someone to be your priority while allowing yourself to be their option."**
>
> MARK TWAIN

If not now, then when? It is very important to seek support. Go to your clergy person, friends and family. Go to a therapist or do family counseling. Let them know how you feel, that you want to change your life.

Keep in mind you need to do what's good for you, not for others. Being in the business of selling real estate, there are countless times I hear that someone who wants to make a change in their lives is stymied by family members not to sell their homes in order to go to alternative housing. Not for the good of the owner but for themselves.

"Oh, no! You can't sell. We have always come down for a week at Christmas time, the kids and we will miss it!" That is not your concern.

I live by the golden rule "Do unto other as you would have them do unto you," and what's even more important now that you are starting this new chapter in your life is, "To thine own self be true." I sincerely care about others and I want this primer to be about helping those men and women who think they can't, to knowing that they can.

THE DIANE KEATON MAKEOVER

We are aging, like every living thing inhabiting the earth. I look like yesterday's wet crepe paper, dried out. Try as we might, DNA, nature, gravity and the environment are foes and resistors of the braking of the aging process. Many days, upon waking up, I have to reintroduce myself to the old lady staring back at me in my bathroom mirror. Sometimes it's my grandmother and, of course, my mother makes frequent mirror appearances. At times it's a complete stranger, and I sure as hell don't know who she is. With so many of us crowding in, I need a bigger bathroom.

Baggy, haggy, and saggy, on various days one or all of these descriptions fit, but there are still days when I can tuck them all out of sight. We do have options. Some of them are quick fixes, like bangs or Botox. The bangs cover the lines in your forehead and Botox will smooth them out for about six months. Google *Restalyne* and *Juvaderm*. These are two of the many wonder management treatments of the twenty-first century, which are good for the body, and therefore good for the mind.

See what works best for you if you choose to go the preservative route. If you think you look good, you will feel good. There are lifts for your face and any other part of your body that needs a pick-me-up. They range from long lasting cut n' tuck procedures, to fillers for instant gratification and the immediate and temporary removal of crow's feet and marionette lines.

There are procedures for whatever troubles us, whether they are real or imagined. If we find something that we perceive mars our self-image, we can revamp it and make it better. If it makes you feel better, then go for it. We have the ability to support or destroy our self-esteem at will. Why do we do this, too many airbrushed role models to compete with, perhaps?

Some of your favorite role models create a picture that is delusional, in not admitting to their fans that it's not merely a combination of good DNA, and the right food and exercise, and that includes men and women, that makes them look like they do. They never admit publicly they have all had "work" done.

Take it from one who has *been there, done that,* they all have had something done. If you have the bucks, plastic surgeons will make the tucks, from your behind, to your flapping arms, to your face.

BTW, there is absolutely NOTHING wrong with letting nature take its course and aging with dignity, think Maggie Smith. Remember "Beauty is in the eyes of the beholder" and you should be the beholder of what makes you feel best.

For God's sake take off all that makeup, unless you like looking like a silly old clown. You may look beautiful in your bathroom, in the morning, but check yourself at noon, outside in the sun. You won't be a happy camper. Mascara, a little blush, a swipe of lipstick, is all you need, and you should be "good to go." You can sport a stylish hair style but kill the spray unless you like looking like you have a frozen nest glued to your scalp. You can check out some of the very chic wigs. They are difficult to distinguish from real hair, with the advantage that they don't have to be sprayed stiff.

Never thin enough, young enough, smart enough, pretty enough, enough is enough. Be careful what you wish for. After the age of sixty, take stock of what and who you are. If you are of average weight, give up trying to lose those extra five or ten pounds.

If you do lose them, (and ultimately find them again like you have been doing for the last fifty years), you will likely lose body fat in your face, which is what's keeping your dimples from turning into wrinkles. If you are on the plump side, stay that way. You made it this far in life and besides, you may be getting to the age when you are too old to die young. Notice the word was *plump*, not fat.

If you are thin, do not get any thinner. Skinny people can look emaciated, especially after a certain age, as the body fat seems to have melted off your bones. What can be detrimental to your health are the ups and downs of weight, or the "yo-yo effect." Like yourself the way you are, others do. Now that you have come to terms with who you are, we can get on with making the best of that.

A *"look"* worth trying is *The Diane Keaton Look,* which consists of a Donna Karan white turtleneck long sleeve cotton shirt with the sleeves long enough to cover the upper part of your hands, casual fitting slacks, low heeled shoes, pearls, and oversized glasses. On some occasions, a hat worn over an above-the-shoulder haircut, with bangs, and a big smile on your face, can add just what is needed to complete the ensemble. Let's call it the divorce with no remorse look. It's perfect for the over sixty group, and besides, it may drive your "frenemies" crazy!

THESE ARE A FEW OF MY FAVORITE THINGS

These are not *Some of My Favorite Things**, but some of the things I did to start acknowledging and accepting is that *You Can't Bring Back Yesterday***.

First, make the best of a bad situation. I found the act of giving or throwing away FLOML's stuff made me feel lighter and happier. Gone are the souvenirs from the road races, which he left behind, as well as multiple shavers, and clothes, including the out of style tuxedo he bought in 1995, and the clothes he chose not to take. He left all of his *don't wants* for me to discard as he packed whatever he wanted to keep for his life's next-to-last journey, like coffee mugs for those special cups of java.

I broke them and threw away the pieces. It was liberating as I felt relief while I was chiseling away and creating distance between us. A chasm was growing deeper and wider as each day passed, he on one side, me on the other. I knew I never wanted to cross the bridgeless span again.

Love songs are written to make you feel romantic. Sad songs pull on your heartstrings. Funny, how songs are popping up that do neither of these, but work for me regardless.

Little did I know that one day I would be singing or humming songs that helped me through the rough stuff. I was in the shower and I started to sing Rogers and Hammerstein's, *I'm Gonna Wash That Man Right Outta My Hair****. It really worked! I cleaned my hair and my head at the same time and got in some secret singing. Of course, who doesn't know the words to *The Sun Will Come Out Tomorrow*, from the Broadway show and movie, *Annie*?

The sun does and will come out even on cloudy days. The sun may not be shining but it is still there, and so are you. *I Pick Myself Off, Dust Myself Off and Start All Over Again*****. Why not let that song from the 40's be a mantra for starting anew?

Go fly a kite, swing on a swing, walk along a sandy shore. Get out there. It's easier than ever. Make a date with yourself. Nothing, and no one, will stop you, but yourself. Everything and anything is there for the taking. Don't rely on someone else to share your space. Ride a bike? Sure, it's easy if that's what you like. In cities all over the country there are bike rental stands. Happy riding.

Go to dinner or have a lunch date with yourself, after all, you are your own best company. When I am asked if I feel comfortable eating alone, I tell them the only time I eat alone is at home, and that's by choice. If you go to restaurants, especially food courts in malls, are you eating alone? There are hundreds of people there.

I am a people watcher and enjoy seeing and hearing bits of conversations from those around me, offering an abundant array of live entertainment. You are not eating alone, there's always your trusty pal, your phone, smart or not. I find it a perfect time to clear out my emails or catch up on *Words with Friends*. Many times, someone will sit near me and start a conversation. You could be that person.

Still can't do it? Don't be afraid to take the next step. Find another lone diner, sit close enough to speak and be heard but not intrusive, and strike up a conversation. Learn some key conversation starting lines, like "Excuse me, maybe you could help me. If you eat pasta and antipasti at the same meal, would you still be hungry?"

You could also ask, "Besides being confronted by a total stranger while enjoying a meal, what are some of your other pet peeves in life?" You may be surprised at what happens next. To be perfectly "frank", if I may, it has been said that people eating alone, sans outside interferences, tend to eat slower and savor their food, thereby enjoying it more, rather than being distracted by conversations which are not always to your liking or approval.

Alone at the movies . . . I don't think so. I like my own space and don't enjoy sitting near someone, who, whether I know them or not, may be slurping on a big drink soda and munching and crunching on a $15.00 container of popcorn. Try going to the movies at off hours.

Tuesday is discount day for seniors at many theaters. Yay! $2.00 off the ticket price and you are in the dark with other mostly singles, enjoying the start of the movie without having so many theatre goers checking one last time to see if that all important message happened before shutting their communication centers down. The rude ones tend to sneak peeks during the show, seemingly oblivious to the bright light shining in others' eyes. Don't be shy to tell them to stop.

You don't like who sat in front, on the side, or behind you? Move. Generally, because the theaters are not full, hence the off hours discounts, you can sit where you want, move if you want, (see above) or if you don't like the movie, leave. Get your money back. It is much more difficult to exert this freedom if you are accompanied by an unwilling companion.

As soon as that other person you are with says, "No" you are stuck. You have forfeited and ceded your vote to the board of directors!

I discovered writing to be restorative. Can't do it or don't want to do it? You decide. Find something else that makes you feel great and do it. Remember everything in life begins with one step. There is a saying, the *Merry Widow*; how about a *Stress-free Single*? I like being with myself when I am at home, but, I know, this is not for everyone.

Involve yourself with new beginnings, i.e., clubs, groups, traveling, religious organizations. Whatever you enjoy and get involved in, you will find other people who share your interests.

There are a multitude of *Meet-Up* groups online, almost everywhere, with interests as varied as hiking, knitting, travel, camping, yoga, reiki or just simple brunch or dinner get togethers. You can choose with whom to interact and have conversations with.

Some will turn out to be worthless, one-time happenings, but some will turn out to be interesting conversations with double-sided attention-grabbing twists and turns, ups and downs, pros and cons, and it will be okay to have different opinions. That's what I'm missing, something that I haven't had for so many years.

I don't even remember when it changed. I am excited and so should you be, about traversing roads yet to be traveled, about talking with people you would never have considered before. It's fun to dream and fantasize, you can do both. You never know when those fantasies will become real. Only then will you discover your dreams becoming reality.

Although it may take a night or two to get comfortable, switch sides in your bed. Not only is it beneficial for you but, being practical, it allows the mattress to wear out more evenly. Believe it or not, it confuses the demons in your head by sleeping in the middle of the bed. Try it, after a night or two you'll find you like it. His and hers, his and his, hers and hers pillows . . . switch them and turn them over, and every night for four nights, you will be sleeping on fresh linens.

If you can't sleep, think about what you've eaten or not eaten in the last few hours. I know I can't sleep when I am hungry. Get up! I'm not saying to make yourself a full course meal. I fry a couple of eggs, put them on a plate, put the plate on a tray, and go back to bed. Prop yourself up, put on the TV, and have a pajama party with your best friend, yourself. Believe it or not you should sleep like a baby after that.

Stop aging! I have decided I am not changing ages every year. Who cares? I'm too old to die young, therefore, from this day on I will always be the age I am today. At any age you can and must stay involved, connected, and excited about reaching out to touch and experience new feelings.

Woody Allen once said, "You can live to be a hundred if you give up all the things that make you want to live to be a hundred." Not so, don't miss anything. You get one shot at life, don't waste it. It really is the trip of a lifetime. We all know there's no going back. As we regrettably recognize later in life, the missed opportunities, the should'ves, could've ones and ohhh, those stories that start with *if only*. Don't miss the next one. I hope I am passing on these feelings to others who will benefit from my observations.

*Julie Andrews song from Sound of Music, written by Richard Rogers

** Song written by Walter Hirsch

***Song from South Pacific by Rogers and Hammerstein

****Song (written by Jerome Kern and Dorothy Fields)

THE HEALTHY BENEFITS OF LAUGHTER IN
YOUR NEW LIFE

A s you find yourself in a new life situation, dealing with all of the nuances, trials, and tribulations of re-formatting your day-to-day existence, take advantage of some of life's more helpful and simple self-aids. No, I'm not talking drugs or alcohol, here. I'm talking about a human being's natural sense of humor. Laughter is a very good thing. Do it often, and never underestimate the power of humor.

One of the best feelings in the world (ranking just below winning the Lotto, and slightly above a warm bath on a cold night) is the release of a good belly laugh. It can bring people together and establish amazing connections. Everything from a slight giggle to a side-splitting hoot can boost the temperature of a room from frosty unfamiliarity to a warm friendly-like atmosphere.

There is much to love about laughter and humor, as well as its natural advantages to our well-being. It has proven to lower blood pressure, and thus, reduce the risk of strokes and heart attacks. It lessens stress hormone levels, which in turn simultaneously cuts anxiety and stress, which impact your body negatively.

Laughing also aids in toning your mid-section, because as you laugh, the muscles in your stomach expand and contract, mimicking the intentional exercise of your abs. Laughter has also been shown to be a wonderful cardiac workout, especially for those who are unable to participate in other physical activities due to injury or illness. Laughter burns the same number of calories per hour as walking at a moderate pace, and you can do it without having to go anywhere.

Another advantage is that it boosts and activates T-cells, which help fight off sickness. Laughter releases endorphins, which are the body's natural pain killers, and in many cases can ease chronic pain throughout the body. Most of all, and ranking high in importance, is laughter's ability to increase your overall sense of well-being. Laughter usually runs hand in hand with a positive outlook on life, which helps to fend off diseases far better than persons who tend to be more negative.

Let us not forget Mel Brooks' explanation of the difference between tragedy and comedy, "Tragedy is when I cut my finger. Comedy is when you fall into an open manhole."

As you saunter from one end to the other, of the temporary obstacle course that has become your new existence, dream of a better tomorrow, where chickens can cross the road and not be questioned about their motives and take a knapsack or jetpack full of laughter along with you. It will make the trip far less hazardous and help to support that new lifestyle you see unfolding in front of you.

> It's amazing how one simple smile can hide all the pain and frustration you're going through.

OPPORTUNITIES

A recent New York Times online article titled, "*The 40-50 Year Itch*", found that many going through divorce after thirty to fifty years of marriage view their circumstances not as a tragedy, but rather as an opportunity. It was found that these "gray divorcees" used words like "freedom", "new choices", and "liberation" when talking about their separation. Others related that they and their partner had simply grown and changed in different ways over the years.

Sometimes their differences are as simple as one person wanting to retire while the other wished to continue working. Of course, there are times, when the differences were not so simple, like "I can't see myself wasting even one more second of my life with you."

Many factors have contributed to the relative ease with which older couples are able to handle divorce. For one, the stigma attached to divorce has faded considerably in our society, due to its frequency, as almost half of all marriages end in divorce. Also, couples at that stage of their lives have usually long since had children grow up and move out. Ok, not always grow up, but at least move out.

It is easier than you think to get started with new opportunities. Ask your friends and acquaintances for suggestions or Google jobs for the over 50 crowd, charities, organizations and volunteering sites. It's a new world out there. Take the first step. If you try something and it's not your thing, that's okay. Quit. Get a job or do volunteer work. If you like to travel, check out the possibilities, such as flight attendant, tour guide, or working on a cruise ship.

The more you look, the more you will see that opportunities are endless, and you can take advantage of what fits your interests. Regardless of how docile or outrageous, what you want to do is, go for it! There are innumerable positives about "gray divorce" that will afford you new opportunities.

You may even start having sex again. The more interesting people you meet, the more you will learn, and, as a result, the more interesting you will become, not only to others, but most importantly, to yourself. You may experience emotions and connections you haven't felt in decades, or perhaps even known before. Sex has added attributes and advantages over and above mere physical pleasure. It is a great boost for the ego, not to mention the aerobic advantages.

Albert Einstein is quoted as saying, "In the middle of chaos, lies opportunity". Your head is spinning, friends and family are all giving you advice, and you are having a difficult time determining which end is up. Why does it seem that some people have all the luck? Unbeknownst to you they are not letting the opportunities out there go by untested. This is the time to seize the opportunity for yourself to make the move into your new zone. Realize you can now be that somebody you always wanted to be.

If you ask baby boomers, and those of the previous generation, why they got married, an absurdly high percentage will offer some version of the following: "Well, we were mid-20s, or even younger, we'd been dating a couple of years, all our friends were getting married, I liked his/her family, I thought he/she would be a good father/mother, it just made sense, so we did, she was pregnant." By getting out of this long term "no longer going anywhere relationship", you get to hit ESC...your own personal reset button.

You're an entirely different person than you were a half a century or more, ago. You have come to know yourself better -- you have a clearer picture of what you want, and don't want out of life, and who you want to be and be with.

Starting over, or resetting, lets you project the *new you* to the world, not the person you've been during your marriage. Perhaps the new you is just the old you that was waiting to wiggle out of a repressed mind. This new you stands a good chance of either finding a new partner, if that is what you are seeking, better suited to the person you are now, or new interests that can be pursued without outside influence or negativity. It is your choice, everything is now your decision.

After so many years, you may not want a new partner. You have become comfortable with yourself, and your new decision-making process. Your married friends will want to live vicariously through you. Whether happily married, miserably married, or Di-Curious (divorce curious) themselves, they're going to want all the details about everything, including the sex, if that is part of your new life, as well as your new acquaintances and interests. Tell them what you want and keep private what you want. Keep them guessing.

If you get to where you thought you wanted to be and find it's not for you . . . forget-about-it! Move on. This is all about you. Your new life is about being in control of yourself. When you are happy, you will affect everyone around you in a positive way. You will be someone people like and want to be with, and that unto itself, is part of rooting yourself into your new zone.

You need to peek around the next corner
You need to stand on your tiptoes
and look over the next hill
You need to soar over the rainbow
to feel the next thrill

Don't ever think it's too late. It's never too late! If you think like that, then, you will miss the boat, and you must admit, you'd rather be sailing on it.

"TO SUCCEED, JUMP AS QUICKLY AT OPPORTUNITIES AS YOU DO AT CONCLUSIONS"
Benjamin Franklin

A FANTASY OF WISTFUL THINKING

M ark Twain once said, "Age is mind over matter. If you don't mind it doesn't matter."

Did you ever fantasize about being an older woman and having an affair with a younger man, a very much younger man? Not too many years ago, I grasped the concept, that I, along with every living soul on this planet, was merely a passenger on the conveyor belt of life.

When I was a very young woman, I was told that the perfect partnership, perfect for sex, that is, was a woman of about seventy years of age, and a nineteen-year-old male. I forget now who told me that, but more than likely, it was a seventy-year-old woman. Since I was never going to ever be that old, I paid absolutely no attention to this revelation, that is, until now.

Well, be careful what you fantasize about, because much of what you can envision can become your reality. "Hello!" *When did this happen? When did I begin to believe this? Do I dare reach out for something so outrageous?* Hey, if the opportunity presents itself, what's to hold you back from trying something new and having the time of your life? I mean, what's the downside?

Once you have shed your marriage skin and the new you has been freed of any and all restraints, be they legal, moral, or emotional, you are free. Free, not only to contemplate the endless possibilities that are available to you, but to actually pursue and act upon them.

You are now flying solo. That is how I feel about being able to move around my world and reach out for anything and everything that is within my scope of possibility. Some of those things may not seem to be reachable immediately, but, with some effort and diligence, who's to say? The sky is the limit.

Sharing with other men and women, who find themselves at a crossroads or have already been there, has opened up a considerable amount of dialogue with them. They feel compelled to want their own stories included for other grey divorcees to become aware of, whether man or woman, gay or straight. They need that encouragement to step outside their comfort, or black and white zone, and see what the world looks like in bright colors.

My friend, Audrey, recently embarked on a new relationship. When she looked in the mirror afterwards, she said that she felt changed, but didn't seem to look any different, other than, perhaps, that smile on her face. Whatever transpires between you and someone else is for you to know and for others, if you desire, to share in those experiences. It most certainly can be an immediate boost to your ego, as well as a quick fix for depression!

Years ago, there were rings to be grabbed as one was riding on a merry-go-round. The one you wanted was the brass ring. If you were lucky enough to grab that glittering prize, you won a free ride. Reach up and grab that ring of life; you will never know that that free ride could turn out to be the best ride of your life.

DAYDREAM BELIEVER

"Dreams must be heeded and accepted.
For a great many of them come true."
~ Paracelsus

Where would we be without our dreams? They are the mode of transportation to what may become our reality. Daydreams can be defined as "a reverie indulged in while either wide or semi-awake." It's easy to write daydreams off as needless distractions that caused you to miss your exit or burn that bagel...but don't. Learn to value your daydreams and appreciate them as a powerful means of escape or let them be your escort to whatever chance get-together you may stumble upon.

There are no explanations for what may happen in your new life. Because of whom I am, and where I find myself in the general cycle of life, there are numerous endeavors and escapades that have not crossed my thought processes for a number of years, or ever for that matter, experiences that will never make my *to do* list. I have absolutely no interest in parachuting out of an airplane, scuba diving ... anywhere, calf roping at a rodeo, or scaling Mt. Everest.

Call me crazy or just plain un-adventurous, but those events just don't grab me. Likewise, sex fits into this category. Or at least it did, until recently. Having had but one "partner" during my entire life, (I know, I know, it's hard to fathom) sex was not on my *To Do* list, bucket, or on any list for that matter.

Recently, an acquaintance of mine, a man some years my junior, agreed to come to my condo and see if he could straighten out an e-mail dilemma I was having. I was unable to sync the two e-mail accounts I have: one for my business, and one personal. Some mail seemed to vanish into the great netherworld of cyber-space, while on its journey from one to the other. I invited him to my home, to which he had never been. After about a half hour of adjustments and whatever else he did technically, the problem seemed to be alleviated and all of my missing e-mail miraculously appeared. I was overjoyed and poured us each a glass of J. Lohr Pinot Noir to celebrate conquering this stressful problem.

It was a beautiful, breezy, balmy afternoon and while reclining on my chaise on my 'Happy Place', my balcony, and enjoying the buzz that I was feeling from my second glass of wine, I fell into an amorous day time dream.

He and I were enjoying the view. Looking east, seeing the azure blue waters of the Atlantic lapping on the beach behind my condo, and to the west, the Intra-Coastal Waterway and the structures of East Hollywood and Hallandale, both spectacular views from the tenth floor. The scent of the fresh sea air and the sounds of the breaking waves were stimulating. He came over and joined me on the chaise. We talked about life in general and each had another glass of wine.

I felt his hand on my neck and shoulders. He began massaging my flesh and muscles, softly, yet firmly with his fingertips, almost off-handedly. It felt good. I said nothing. A short time later, his hands moved slowly down my back, softly pressing and rubbing along my spine and shoulder blades.

It still felt good, and my silence sent signals that allowed him to continue. He asked me if I wanted to lie down and assured me I would enjoy his massage.

The Pinot, seemingly building up my nerve, I suggested we move to the bedroom. For twenty minutes, he relaxed all the muscles of my body, from my neck, down both sides of my spine, over the backs of my thighs, to my calves, and finally my feet. I hadn't felt this calm, un-wound, and loose in eons. It must have been the wine. Yeah, right. In this dream it could have been Mountain Dew, and it still would have felt great.

My sleep went deeper as I dreamt on. I wasn't sure if I was being too forward, as my dating and intimacy experiences with men has been rather limited to the point of non-existence for the past half century. He told me to get comfortable, leaving me to decipher his definition of comfortable.

I headed for my bathroom, and in a few minutes, returned to the bedroom wearing my bra and panties, which, I soon determined, was coincidentally similar to his present manner of dress. Not a bra and panties mind you, which would have definitely killed the entire scene, but undressed except for his Calvin's.

I lay down on the bed. He continued to massage my back, neck, and legs. It was so relaxing and stress relieving. I could hear myself "Ahhh-ing", out loud, numerous times. Ten minutes later, he asked me to turn over. After mulling this request over in my mind for a good second and a half, I complied. I was tingling. My body was alive. I looked up at him and followed his eyes as he scanned me like a late-night TV host reading cue cards. From top to bottom, and back to the top again, and finally, coming to rest at my center. I decided, then and there, to just become a passenger on this road to who-knows-where and let him take the wheel. He turned out to be an adept driver.

He whispered to me that my pleasure was his pleasure, which made me think, *Wow, he must be feeling really good right now.* My own pleasure peaked a number of times in the next half hour, and after he "peaked", we lay there on our backs, next to each other, as quiet as I am sure is the surface of the moon. You could have heard a bra drop.

He then spoke and told me that this has been a most unexpected and beautiful way to spend a morning and start a day. I concurred with his observation. As a matter of fact, the sex was so good that even the neighbors had a cigarette. He laid my hand on his chest and I felt his heart beating. He informed me that in addition to this being unexpected and beautiful, it was also a wonderfully aerobic experience. I complied fully. We lay there for another half hour and talked. I had to leave for work, and he had to go, too. We got dressed and promised we would get together again.

I awoke from my beguiling dream, momentarily perplexed by the fact that I was no longer on my balcony, but rather, laying in my bed fully dressed for work. I must have had a third glass of wine and not remembered moving or changing. I began to realize there was much more of life I was missing, and my bucket list still had miles to go before being filled, or as Henry David Thoreau so elegantly put it, "Go confidently in the direction of your dreams, and live the life you have imagined."

RECENT TRUISMS REGARDING "GRAY DIVORCE"

Much has been learned in the past few decades about elder divorce, due to the rising numbers of elderly and long term married couples calling it quits. Older couples face unique age-related issues that can factor into the decision to divorce.

These include, but are not limited to, health concerns, tensions brought on by living in closer proximity in retirement, losing parents and friends, and even the unsettling loss of youth. Age and too much togetherness can also bring about more criticism, defensiveness and/or contempt. Why should one tolerate that?

In my situation it was some of the above, but when all was said and done it was just too long to be married. Instead of growing together we were glowering and growling at each other on a constant basis. As Sarah Brightman sings, *Time to Say Goodbye.*

Our lengthening life expectancies decrease the likelihood that marriages will end as your wedding vows says, *til'death do you part,* as was the norm for so many previous generations.

STATS

Couples divorce later in life for the same reasons younger couples split up: infidelity, financial pressures, regrets about earlier decisions, or a desire for greater independence. But when you're over fifty, these reasons are framed by aging and the realization that you have more years behind you than ahead of you. Sociologists are referring to this increase of elder divorce syndrome as the "Gray Divorces Revolution (GDR). You might even call them *Silver Splitters.*

The overall national divorce rates have spiked for the gray (or elder) divorces. At a time when divorce rates for other age groups have stabilized or dropped, fully one out of every four people experiencing divorce in the United States is 50 or older, and nearly one in 10 is 65 or older. Our lengthening life expectancies decrease the likelihood that marriages will end through death.

Many older divorcées say they are happy. According to a 2021 AARP survey, 80% considered themselves, on a scale from 1 to 10, to be on the top half of life's ladder. A majority of 56% even considered themselves to be on the uppermost rung (8-10).

Many two income couples share expenses, but if one does not have to depend on the other for financial security why stay in a relationship that does not bring you pleasure? We are living longer. Don't you want to live happier?

THE SUPPORT TEAM

My three 'Weil' cousins Judy, Laney, and Michael are the Weil's who kept this bus from spinning out of control. Our mothers were sisters, and the daughters of our grandparents, Max and Jennie Weil.

Judy Fryer
An amazing person who knows how to keep everything in perspective. When I wanted to fly away, she made sure my feet stayed anchored to the ground. She showed me how life and lies are like peeling an onion, without me shedding a tear.

Laney Rosenzweig
My 'go to' for everything cerebral. Whenever I wanted to say something, write something, send something, or do something outrageous she stopped me, brought me down to earth and made sure I stayed there.

Michael Levy

A consummate lawyers' lawyer. When Brett said he and Michael were
on the same page they were, however, Michael wrote the book. Without
my Weil cousins, I would not be where I am now, nor would I have able
to say "Happily ever after".

Brett Schultz

My attorney, who when I told him "I don't fuckin' get it" every time he
called me with another dispute, took it – from me. Sorry about that
Brett but that's why you got the big bucks

Elyane Encaoua

She was there for my meltdowns. As I was melting down she was
keeping me cool. She was by my side every step of the way making sure I
stayed erect, looking straight ahead.

Terry Mansky

My friend since elementary school, who encouraged me to write.
Without that support I never would have done what I did. She encouraged me after reading some things that I had written, mostly obits or
letters to Abbey. I guess I can say that this is my last hurrah the ultimate
obit, my own.

AND IN CLOSING

Be Happy! When all is said and done, and you are still with me, what I want you to take away from this primer is knowing you have choices that will make you a better, more fulfilled person, one who does not need another to make you happy.

I'd much prefer to be a fun *one* than half of a dismal two. In life, being number one equates to being the winner, and you, right now, are a winner. Ressies, a party of one, key word being *party*. Go out into the world respecting and knowing you are one whole person who doesn't have to endure another to complete you.

You may, when you least expect it, meet someone you want to be with, great! Learn from your past, don't lose your identity. You may become a committee of two but this time with your vote equal to another.

Being cast away does not mean you're a castaway. Build your life and do it your way. Endless choices are there for the pickings. No longer are you compelled to do what you don't want to do, when you don't want to do it. Get out and get going.

Eons ago, on a trip to Beijing we stayed at the Peninsula Hotel. In the quiet evening I walked outside towards the end of the block. The street was dark and secluded, but not threatening. I got to the end and turned left. I was surprised to see an enormous, full of life, bustling pedestrian mall. Get out, turn the corner and find your own surprises.

Good bye and have a great life! XOXO Brenda.

Soar solo on the soft southern breeze, successfully single.

Please take a moment to rate and or review this book on your favorite book site. Reviews help independent writers attract new readers. Your input is appreciated.

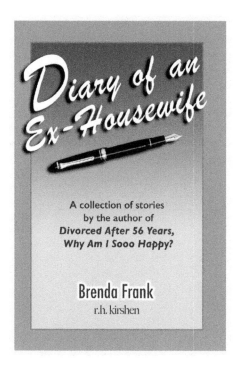

Wonderful, a modern declaration of independence! Dr. J PhD

All divorced women should read this hilarious but wise message and learn to anticipate each day with exciting hopeful joy. Dr. B. Perri PhD

After reading *Divorced After 56 Years, Why am I Sooooo Happy,* readers wanted to know . . . "Where is she now?"

"I'm heeere!"

I stepped out into the world and entered a new life full of adventure as a party of one.

Travel with me in my adventures and misadventures as a single senior enjoying the rest and best of my life.